LIFE ON A
CORAL
REEF

This edition produced
in **1995** for
Shooting Star Press Inc
Suite 1212
230 Fifth Avenue
New York, NY 10001

© Aladdin Books Ltd 1989

Created and produced by
Aladdin Books Ltd
28 Percy Street
London W1P 9FF

*First published in the
United States in 1989 by*
Gloucester Press

ISBN 1-57335-159-8

Printed in Belgium

Design David West
Children's Book Design
Illustrations Stella Robinson
Picture Research Cecilia Weston-Baker
Editor Scott Steedman

This book is about coral reefs and the different animals and plants that live on them. It tells you how coral reefs form, what they look like, and what sort of communities develop around them. You can find out some surprising facts in the boxes on each page. The identification chart at the back of the book will show you some coral reef animals.

The little squares show you the size of the plant or animal, compared to a person.

The picture opposite shows two starfish on a coral reef in Kenya

✱ FIRST SIGHT ✱
LIFE ON A
CORAL
REEF

Lionel Bender

SHOOTING STAR PRESS

Introduction

Corals are tiny marine animals. They have soft bodies and tentacles, like sea anemones. There are about 2,500 different kinds of coral in the world. All of them produce some sort of outer skeleton to live in. Some corals are solitary, but most of them live in large colonies. The skeletons of these colonial corals gradually build up into huge underwater rocky ridges, or reefs.

Coral reefs can grow to be hundreds of feet thick and many hundreds of miles long. They provide a home for all kinds of marine creatures. These attract other animals in turn, creating a rich wildlife community. Some creatures, such as starfish, feed on the corals themselves. Others, like sharks, hunt the small fish and shellfish that teem in the warm reef waters.

Contents

◁ **Shoals of fish find plenty of food around a coral reef**

What is coral?

There are two types of coral. "Hard" corals produce an outer skeleton of calcium carbonate (limestone). In large amounts this forms solid chunks of rock. "Soft" corals have a skeleton of horny tubes, spikes, and rods. These are buried inside the animals' bodies.

Each reef-building coral is about 5 mm (1/5 inch) long. It begins life as a tiny larva that swims freely in the water. When it reaches a firm support, it develops tentacles and an outer skeleton. The tentacles bear stinging cells, which are mainly used to capture small animals to eat. As the coral grows, it produces "buds," as a flower does. These stay attached to the parent. Gradually a huge, spreading colony develops from this budding.

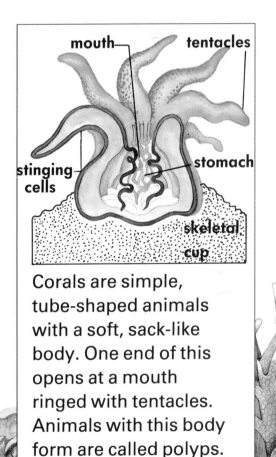

Corals are simple, tube-shaped animals with a soft, sack-like body. One end of this opens at a mouth ringed with tentacles. Animals with this body form are called polyps.

7

Amazing shapes and colors

Stag's Horn, Sea Fan, and Dead Man's Fingers are just a few of the names used to describe the strange shapes of reef corals. Black Corals form slender, branching structures with thorns that are painful to the touch. The polyps in Brain Corals grow in rows. They form a skeleton with ridges and deep, curling grooves that look like the ones on the outside of the human brain.

Most hard corals are white, taking their color from their limestone skeletons. Soft corals are often brightly colored. One type of Red Coral, Corallium, produces deep-red spikes that are used in jewelry. Blue Coral gets its color from special chemicals in the animal's stomach. Sea Fans produce red, green, and blue rods.

Hard coral polyps spread out their tentacles to catch food

. This Brittle Starfish is clambering over a colony of Precious Red Coral ▷

Reef-building

The Great Barrier Reef in Australia is the largest coral reef in the world. It is more than 2,000 km (1,200 miles) long, and probably took several million years to develop. Coral reefs grow at a rate of about 15 cm (6 inches) a year. As old corals die, new ones settle and develop on the surface of their skeletons. Often many different types of coral grow together. Other animals and plants contribute to the structure of the reef. Mussels fill crevices between the corals, and seaweed cements together loose coral sands and shells.

Reef-building corals only grow in clean, clear oceans where the water temperature is above 20° C (68° F). For this reason coral reefs are only found in the Tropics, the warm seas close to the Equator. They thrive in surface waters down to 45 m (150 ft). Beyond this depth there is not enough light for the tiny plants that live within each polyp. These plants are needed for skeleton-building.

Coral reefs usually form around an island that is sinking. They first form a "fringe" close to the shore (1). As the island sinks further, a barrier reef forms (2). A broad stretch of sea separates it from the mainland. When the island disappears completely a circular reef, or atoll, is left (3).

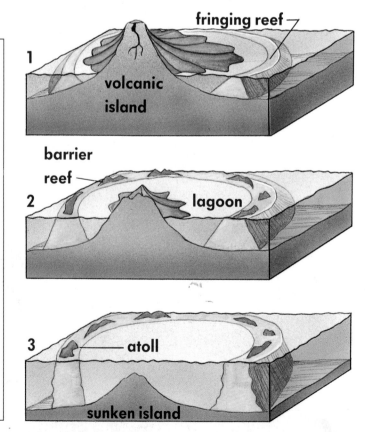

Light penetrates the clear waters above colonies of Stag's Horn Coral ▷

Food chains

All reef animals ultimately depend on plants for food. Water plants are eaten by small animals and fish. These range from the tiny Butterfly Fish the size of your little finger to Basking Sharks 12 m (40 ft) long. Many small fish are hunted by large predators like Barracuda and squid. Or they may be eaten by scavengers, like lobsters, rays, and sea snakes, after they die.

Corals are also part of the food chain. They feed at night, emerging from their skeletal cups and stretching out their tentacles. Small fish, crabs or microscopic animals that collide with the tentacles are paralyzed. They are then trapped and brought to the mouth. Feeding corals are preyed upon in turn. Parrot Fish bite off and eat living chunks of the reef, and starfish rasp away at the soft parts of corals with the suckers on their arms.

Damselfish swim among the coral

Hammerhead Sharks are fierce predators at the top of the coral reef food chain ▷

Ready to pounce

Octopuses and eels lurk in holes and crevices in the reef. They wait for prey to swim by and then shoot out to seize it. Octopuses rely heavily on vision to find and home in on their victims, which include crabs, lobsters, and fish. When they have ambushed an animal, they give it a poisonous bite with their horny jaws. Then they take it back to their hideout to eat. Sometimes octopuses stalk their prey. They swim and crawl over the reef with their eight tentacles, each of which is lined with suckers.

Moray Eels also prey on small fish, crabs, and lobsters. They catch these with their long, thin, razor-sharp teeth. These are hinged so that prey can enter the throat, but can't get out.

A Moray Eel lunges at a passing fish

Moray Eels have a reputation for fierceness. People claim that they prey on divers, inflicting a poisonous bite and never letting their victims escape. In fact, most are not poisonous and their teeth are small.

14

An octopus in a reef crevice ▷

Coral Trout

Cardinal Fish

Beaked Leatherjacket

Shoal of Moorish Idols
Moorish Idols, like many reef fish, live in large groups called shoals. A predator finds it difficult to single out one fish from the shoal. Each fish's chance of being caught is small.

Clownfish

Parrotfish

Red Fire Fish

Defensive tactics

Many reef fish are brightly colored. But the patterns of their coloration help to camouflage them. This protects them from predators. Cardinal Fish, for example, are reddish with black stripes. They are most active at night, spending the daylight hours among corals where their colors blend in well.

Puffer Fish rely on spines to defend themselves. When threatened, they fill their stomachs with water or air to inflate themselves like a balloon. This makes their long, sharp spines stick out. At the same time, their eyes take on a glaring look, which adds to their threatening appearance.

Two Pufferfish, the top one inflated, the other one relaxed ▷

Microscopic life

Billions of tiny plants, known as phytoplankton, drift near the ocean surface above and around coral reefs. Microscopic animals, the zooplankton, graze on them. These range from single-celled creatures that move by lashing their tiny "flagella" (tails), to the larvae (young) of barnacles and snails. Many plankton have gas-filled chambers or oil droplets to help them float.

During the day, phytoplankton use sunlight to convert chemicals and water into food materials. At night they use the food to grow and multiply. Each day at sunset, many of the zooplankton swim to the surface of the water to feed on the plants. At sunrise, they stop feeding and return to deeper water. This gives the phytoplankton time to regrow.

Daily migrations of zooplankton

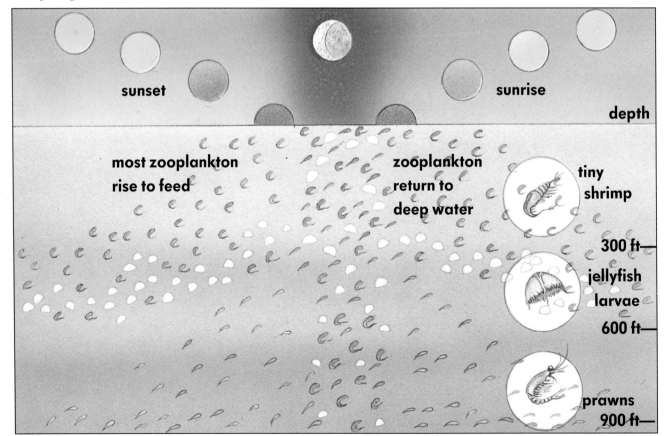

sunset

sunrise

depth

most zooplankton rise to feed

zooplankton return to deep water

tiny shrimp

300 ft—

jellyfish larvae

600 ft—

prawns 900 ft—

The tiny animals, or zooplankton, in a drop of reef water ▷

Lobsters and crabs

The largest lobster in the world lives on coral reefs off the coast of America. It grows as long as 60 cm (2 ft) and weighs up to 20 kg (44 lb). Like all lobsters it is a scavenger. It has four pairs of spindly legs, and scurries across the seabed in search of food. These days few lobsters live long enough to grow very large. They are considered a food delicacy by many people and are caught in great numbers.

The Japanese Spider Crab is even bigger – its outstretched legs span almost 8 m (26 ft). This crab lives on the sandy bottoms close to reefs, where it feeds on shrimp, starfish, worms, and clams. Like the lobster, it has a hard jointed "armour" – called an exoskelton – that protects it from predators.

Migrating Spiny Lobsters

Spiny Lobsters live on reefs off Florida and the Caribbean. In the fall they migrate south to warmer waters, traveling up to 15 km (9 miles) a day. They move in single file, one behind the other, using sight and touch.

Two reef crabs, the Australian Coral Crab...

...and the Splendid Coral Crab

21

Turtles

Sea turtles like the Green and Loggerhead swim huge distances across the tropical seas. They often stop at coral reefs to feed and rest. The Green Turtle, for example, is a frequent visitor to reefs off the coasts of East Africa, Indonesia, Australia, and South America. It is a plant-eater that comes to feed on seaweed in the shallow waters. But the Loggerhead and most other sea turtles are meat-eaters. They prey on jellyfish, crustaceans, mussels, sea urchins, and fish.

Like all reptiles, sea turtles breathe air using lungs and lay eggs that have leathery shells. Though they mate in the water, the females must come ashore to lay their eggs. Female Green Turtles often lay their eggs on island beaches in the Great Barrier Reef.

Young turtles dashing for the sea

Green Turtle

As soon as baby sea turtles hatch they head for the open water. On the way, most are gobbled up by birds, crabs and lizards. Those that survive spend years at sea.

Hawksbill Turtle off the coast of Florida ▷

Sea snakes and starfish

Sea snakes feed on the fish eggs and eels found on coral reefs. The largest species, the Banded Sea Snake, grows to 2.5 m (8.5 ft) long. They are all related to cobras and kill quickly using a powerful poison. But sea snakes can't move well on land and don't come ashore to lay eggs. Instead, most give birth to live young in the water.

Most starfish have five arms, though some have as many as 40. The arms spread out from a central body. If one arm is lost, a new one grows in its place. Starfish use their arms to pry open mussel and clam shells. The Crown-of-thorns Starfish also uses them to prey on coral polyps. This does great damage to the reefs.

A Crown-of-thorns Starfish feeds on coral polyps

An Olive Sea Snake hunting on a reef ▷

Fan worms and sea slugs

Fan worms get their name from their brightly colored and feathery tentacles. They use these to breathe and feed. Their diet is mostly small animals and floating particles of food, which they filter from the reef water with their outstretched fans. The worms produce a hard, outer tube which protects their bodies as they grow. When they rest or are threatened, the animals disappear inside the tube. A structure like a plug in the center of the fan seals the entrance.

Sea slugs are related to snails. But most species do not have a shell. They swim over reefs with wave-like movements of their flattened bodies. Many sea slugs prey on jellyfish and sea anemones. They then use their victims' stinging cells to defend themselves.

The Spanish Dancer, a colorful sea slug

A fan worm opens its tentacles to feed ▷

Coral reefs are constantly building up and wearing away. New polyps are always developing, and coral colonies growing larger. But at the same time predators and the action of waves and wind work to destroy reefs. These opposing processes have been going on for millions of years, though in recent times human interference has upset the balance of nature. Pollution of the water, dredging, blasting and drilling for minerals and oil, the greenhouse effect, the hole in the ozone layer, tourism — all are threatening to destroy coral reefs faster than they can grow.

A sea turtle is cut open for its eggs and meat

Pollution affects coral reefs in various ways. Sewage and toxic waste either poison the coral polyps or kill the zooplankton on which they feed. Pesticides from the land and oil from spills can damage reefs in the same ways. Sediments and sand cloud the water, preventing light from reaching the tiny plants which live inside the polyps. This is fatal for the polyps – and the reef.

Blasting and drilling for minerals and oil around coral reefs can have disastrous effects. Coral is broken up and the local ecology disrupted. Plant life is also killed, threatening the survival of the animals that depend on them. The greenhouse effect – a warming of the Earth's atmosphere – is also a serious threat. This has already led to worldwide rises in sea levels, which are likely to continue. The harm done to reef life could be huge.

Tourism also threatens reef communities. Divers damage living polyps and remove chunks of coral for souvenirs or to make jewelry. Probably the best protection is to make reefs into wildlife reserves. In 1975, the Australian government declared the Great Barrier Reef a Marine Park. Parts of the reef are now "no-go" areas for anyone except scientists, who need to study corals and the wildlife around them.

Oil pollutes coral reef water

A Crown-of-thorns Starfish

We can explore reefs without damaging them

Identification chart

Some of the many animals found on coral reefs are shown here. The grid is divided into 15 cm (6 inch) squares. Many of these animals can be seen in a marina, and some you can keep in a home aquarium. If you visit a coral reef, be sure not to damage the coral or disturb the animals that live on and around the reef.

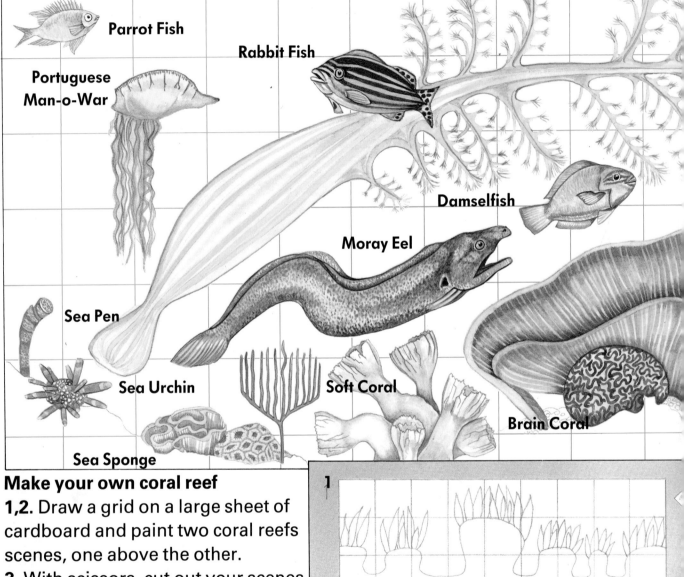

Parrot Fish

Rabbit Fish

Portuguese Man-o-War

Damselfish

Moray Eel

Sea Pen

Sea Urchin

Soft Coral

Brain Coral

Sea Sponge

Make your own coral reef

1,2. Draw a grid on a large sheet of cardboard and paint two coral reefs scenes, one above the other.

3. With scissors, cut out your scenes.

4. With more cardboard, make a window-folder and stick one of your reef scenes in it.

5. Mount your second scene on a card with a pull tab at the top.

6. Pull the tab-card in and out to create a moving image.

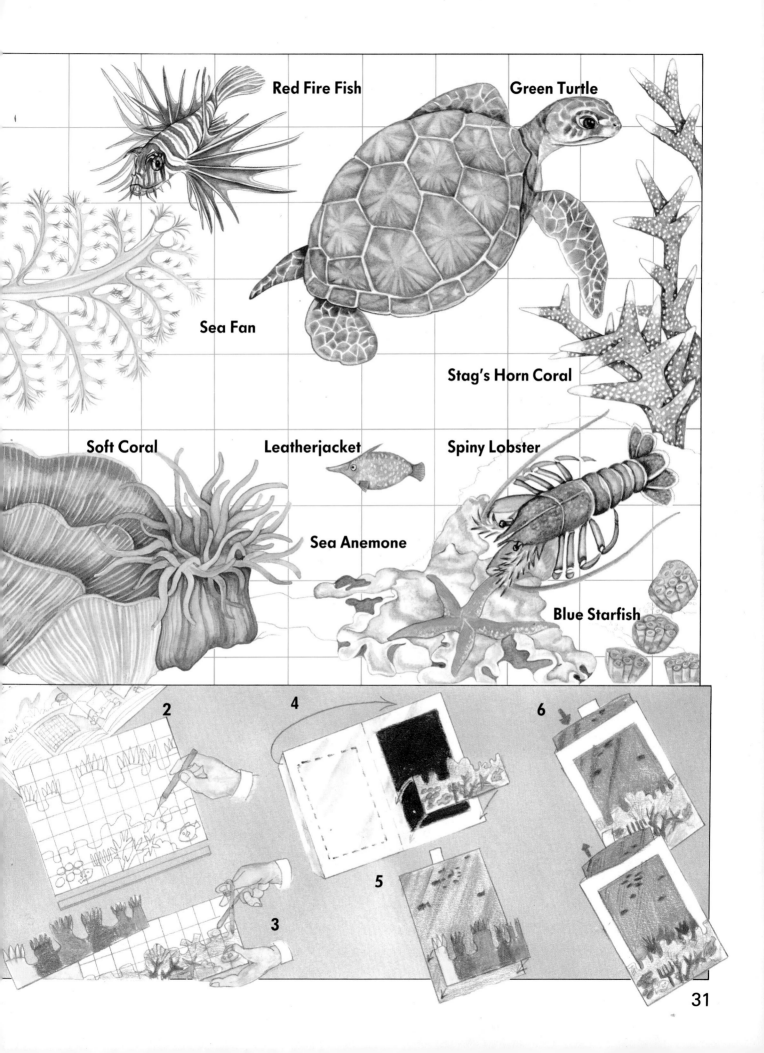

Red Fire Fish

Green Turtle

Sea Fan

Stag's Horn Coral

Soft Coral

Leatherjacket

Spiny Lobster

Sea Anemone

Blue Starfish

2

4

6

3

5

Index

Photographic Credits: Cover and pages 4, 6, 9, 12, 13, 15, 19, 23, 26 and 29 all: Planet Earth; title page and pages 8, 11, 17, 21 both, 24, 27, and 28: Bruce Coleman; page 25: Robert Harding Library.